The Unused Path

Skills for living an authentic life

Vincent H. O'Neil

ISBN 978-1-7378245-0-3

Novels by Vincent H. O'Neil

A Pause in the Perpetual Rotation

The Interlands horror series
Interlands
Denizens

Murder mysteries
Death Troupe
Crime Capsules
Murder in Exile (Frank Cole #1)
Reduced Circumstances (Frank Cole #2)
Exile Trust (Frank Cole #3)
Contest of Wills (Frank Cole #4)

Science Fiction written as Henry V. O'Neil
Glory Main (Sim War #1)
Orphan Brigade (Sim War #2)
Dire Steps (Sim War #3)
CHOP Line (Sim War #4)
Live Echoes (Sim War #5)

www.vincenthoneil.com

Why the unused path?

This book is called The Unused Path for several reasons.

Paths lead from one place to another. This work contains advice and practical approaches you might find useful on your life journey.

The path is unused because a good deal of the information in this book isn't emphasized as much as it once was. Most of the advice and the skills offered here have been circulating for a very long time. They're fundamental and valuable but, like so many worthwhile concepts in this increasingly technological age, they can get overlooked in the competition for our attention.

That doesn't mean the path's irrelevant, or that it's gone. A path that isn't used becomes overgrown, but it's still there even if it's not easy to see.

This path is still there because it leads toward a valuable destination—the living of an authentic life you can truly call your own.

Let's walk some of it now.

Author's Note

This work is a companion to my futuristic fiction novel *A Pause in the Perpetual Rotation*. Although this book is featured prominently in that novel, it is a non-fiction work in its own right that is intended to offer good advice and sound approaches for building an authentic life.

One of the primary principles of The Unused Path is that each of us is unique. That means there is no way to tailor the advice in this book to fit every individual who reads it.

Please feel free to modify the suggestions in this work to suit your own circumstances, abilities, and needs. Do not follow any of these suggestions if doing so would place you or anyone else in any kind of danger.

In addition to helpful observations and sound advice, this book offers concrete skills for approaching a wide range of choices and issues we may encounter in life. These techniques are intentionally basic, and this book does not pretend to contain all the answers.

Instead, this work is a starting point that will hopefully help you find, choose, or create your own path leading to an authentic existence.

The Unused Path

Take a moment

This book begins with a question:

Whose life are you going to live?

The discussion of this question starts on the next page, but take some time now to consider it.

What does this question mean?

What does it mean to you?

How would you answer it?

Give it some thought, because it's a bit of a trick question.

Whose life are you going to live?

Whose life are you going to live?

Yours.

That's a simple fact. No matter who or what chooses the things you'll do in life, that life is going to be lived by you.

That means you will personally experience the successes and the failures, the high points and the low, the accolades and the criticisms.

This does not mean you should ignore the advice of others and rely only on yourself. Nor does it suggest you should live a life dedicated only to your concerns.

It means that, whatever life you lead, you should be the one who chooses it.

After all, you're the one who's going to live it.

Living an authentic life

When something is authentic, it's not false or imitation. It is genuine.

If you let other people and random circumstances choose your beliefs, actions, and attitudes, you might end up with a life that doesn't fit you or your personality. If you're the one who makes those choices, however, you may just end up living authentically. Your actions, words, and thoughts will match who you are. They will be genuine.

Leading an authentic existence can help you to weather the storms that life throws at all of us. It's easy to lose your bearings in difficult circumstances, but if you know who you are and what you value, the experience of living the life you choose will help you stay on course.

This doesn't mean you should be selfish or self-centered. You can serve others. You can include them in your life. You can take advice from people you trust. The point is that you actually choose the existence you lead.

Defining your authentic life is a never-ending process, because we all change as we go down the road. We adjust our attitudes based on experiences and new information—which can lead to true wisdom.

Making choices

Every life is different. That includes the degree to which we're able to select what we do. Many decisions are made for us by circumstances and by events beyond our control. Even if you aren't given a whole lot of choices in this life, it's important to make good decisions when you can.

A little later we'll explore a basic approach for identifying different options and making informed choices. Along the way, we'll also discuss how you can find reliable sources of guidance, information, and example that can help you decide what you'll do in a given set of circumstances.

None of those approaches is meant to take the place of your own common sense and the information you gather with your own eyes and ears. If you can develop sound judgement regarding the advice of others and your own thought process, you'll have the tools to recognize good information and create solid options from it.

Now let's take a look at how we might start honing that judgement.

Develop your mind—always

Not surprisingly, there are many definitions of the human mind.

One definition calls the mind the human consciousness that originates in the brain and is manifested in thought, perception, feeling, will, memory, or imagination.

For our purposes, your mind is the combination of who you are and how you navigate the world around you. Your mind is unique, and it improves with learning. That learning can be gained through your own experiences or from the knowledge you get from others.

Think of your mind as your command center as you go through life. Your command center takes in information and makes judgements and decisions about those inputs based on what you've learned beforehand. Receiving too many inputs at once, or getting conflicting information, can lead to confusion.

This has always been true, but in our modern age we're subjected to a flood of images and ideas that is larger, more constant, and more demanding than ever before.

So let's discuss some approaches for dealing with that huge amount of information.

The world is a classroom

If reading the word "classroom" made you roll your eyes, this section of the book is for you.

Knowledge can be obtained in countless ways. To name just a few, we can learn by attending school-style classes, reading the written words of others, interacting with more knowledgeable people, viewing instructional media such as informative videos, performing new tasks, or thinking things over ourselves.

Additionally, we can learn a great deal simply by being alive. Everyday life is packed with reliable and unreliable information, good and bad examples, sound and unsound advice, and experiences from which we can glean both knowledge and wisdom if we just pay attention.

That's how the first human beings learned. Before there were classrooms, books, teachers, or videos they learned by observing and by doing. They advanced through trial and error, and developed effective methods and answers because there was no one to show or tell them how.

The way they did it has been with us ever since. It worked for them, and it's an excellent foundation. The world is a classroom.

Time is a resource

As promised in the book's introduction, this work offers a range of specific skills that can be of great value as you go through life. They can help you organize your thoughts and actions, manage your time and your money, and solve complex problems. They're fundamental skills for getting things done.

Something that is fundamental serves as a foundation for greater growth and development. The examples in this work are relatively simple, but with a little imagination every one of the skills covered here can be applied on a larger scale. Individual techniques of time management—which we'll discuss next—can easily be taught to a group or used for managing a project.

We're starting with time management because it has such a wide application to so much of what we do. There's a limited amount of time in each working day and before every deadline. Sometimes there simply isn't enough time to accomplish everything on the list.

Time is therefore a resource. A resource is anything that we use in order to accomplish a task, and so it's important to manage our resources wisely.

Time management

Prioritization

Consider the list of everything you need to do today. If all the tasks on that list are equal in importance, it's difficult to choose which one to do first. Not all jobs or chores are equal, and so one way to approach time management is to prioritize our list of tasks.

What does that mean? We start by examining each task in terms of impact and urgency. Obviously, picking up a child from school ranks higher than picking up the dry cleaning. In this approach, we may not accomplish every job on the list—but we will complete the important ones.

Assigning importance to a task is a good start, but there's more to prioritization than that. If we notice that we have two related chores on the list and that one can't be started before the other is completed, that's a prioritization too. For example, if your list has you dropping off a donation of canned goods at a charity drive but also buying those goods, you'll obviously have to go to the store first.

There can be other reasons for a task's ranking on the list. If we promised someone we'd get a specific job done by the end of the day, it receives a higher prioritization even if it's not terribly urgent.

Time management
Scheduling

This approach is easier than prioritization, because parts of it are done for us. Some tasks, such as an appointment with a doctor, are easier to manage because they already have an assigned date and time. This is especially true of recurring events such as a weekly meeting. We have to attend the meeting, so it goes on the schedule and our other tasks have to work around it.

The specific characteristics of a task can also dictate its scheduling. Let's say you noticed your weekly grocery shopping takes much less time if you go on a Wednesday night. It could be scheduled whenever you're free, but doing it on Wednesday night is a more efficient use of your time.

Another example of this approach takes location into account. If you have tasks on the list that require you to go different places, analyzing those locations can suggest a time-saving step. Schedule those chores that occur in the same general area so that you only have to go there once.

Time management
Duration

All the prioritization and scheduling in the world won't make much difference if we don't know how much time a given task is likely to take. Underestimate the duration of a project, and it may run over into other scheduled events. Overestimate how long a task will run, and you may end up with unused time that was unnecessarily reserved for that job that could have been used elsewhere.

This approach highlights some of the skills we've already discussed. Paying attention to the world around you can provide insights and prior warning about the holdups and obstacles you may encounter. Your own experiences can serve as a yardstick for the rate at which you work and how much time certain tasks require.

Although overestimating how long a task takes can often waste time, don't be afraid to add some wiggle room to a plan so you have some flexibility if a job gets delayed. Additionally, when you're planning a series of activities that run back-to-back, consider plugging some open time in between them for cleanup, review of the work, and rest.

Gaining Fundamentals

What are fundamentals?

There are many definitions of this term. For our purposes, fundamentals are skills or characteristics that can form a foundation on which other things are built.

For example, in team competitive sports there are usually sets of basic individual skills that each player must master just to be considered for inclusion on the team. The team itself has basic group skills it must be able to execute before it can progress to learning more advanced plays and formations. Those are fundamentals.

Just because something is basic doesn't mean it's simple or easy. In the field of medicine, complete knowledge of human anatomy is considered a prerequisite. Anyone who has memorized the proper names for every part of the body can tell you it is not simple or easy.

While you're determining what it means for you to live an authentic life, you'll be identifying fundamental attitudes, values, and behaviors that match or define who you are. The next few pages are a discussion of some of those characteristics that you may already have or may decide to adopt. Feel free to adjust them as you see fit.

Treat others as you'd be treated

This ancient piece of advice is also known as The Golden Rule: Do unto others as you would have done unto you.

It's a complete philosophy of life in one sentence, and it makes sense.

To guide our actions toward others, we need only look at our own reactions to different experiences.

If we don't like it when someone steals our belongings, then we shouldn't take what doesn't belong to us. The same approach works when we consider our reactions to people gossiping about us, cheating us, or assaulting us.

Likewise, we should consider adopting the behaviors that we admire in others. If we appreciate it when people are helpful, we should try to act that way ourselves. The same approach works when we consider our reactions to people who respect our privacy, keep their word, or show simple courtesy.

Listen and pay attention

This one's a combination of learning just by being alive and treating others the way we'd like to be treated. When someone's talking to you, they're giving information or trying to get information. If we aren't listening, we may miss a valuable insight or fail to assist someone who's asking us for something.

This is more easily said than done. Our brains never shut off, and they process all of the inputs we receive as we get them. Along with the words coming from the individual speaking to us, we're also receiving sensory inputs from our surroundings. While all this is happening, we have our own concerns and tasks on our minds.

We can all benefit from improving our listening skills. Start by noticing how much or how little you're retaining from the conversations you have. Notice how many times your mind wanders to a topic that seems more important or more interesting. Gauge how often you're formulating your next comment instead of hearing what's being said.

When we pay closer attention, we're more present in an interaction. It's thoughtful, polite, and a good discipline.

Eyes and ears open—brain engaged

We can learn something from most situations, no matter how mundane. Everyday life is filled with opportunities to hone our minds, and all we have to do is pay attention.

When you can, take some time to watch what's going on around you. Don't be rude and don't make anyone feel uncomfortable, but casually take it all in.

Practice observing activity without drawing conclusions. It's harder than it sounds. See what's happening, but don't try to make sense of it at first. This approach can prevent our assumptions from influencing our observations.

Much of the time, what you observe will explain itself. The nervous man standing near a lobby entrance suddenly brightens up when the late package he's been waiting for arrives. The bird that repeatedly flies into view and back out, never using the same approach but always landing in the same tree, is greeted by tiny chirps from a nest it was concealing by its movements. You figured all of that out just by watching and listening.

Being actively present puts us in greater touch with our surroundings, can help us synch up with our environment, and can teach us things as well.

What are you trying to do?

This is one of the key questions in life. It can be posed at a very high level ("What am I trying to do with my life?") or the very specific ("What am I trying to accomplish in this chore?") and we should ask it often.

Have you ever started a task without having a solid idea of what you were supposed to accomplish? Ever worked on a job where the directions kept changing? If we don't know what we're trying to achieve before we start, we're likely to waste a lot of effort or even fail.

It's not enough to know what we're trying to do—we also have to know what it means to reach the finish line. In other words, what exactly do we have to do before we can say we're done?

That question has even more benefits, because it makes us ask how we're going to approach this task. Are we able to achieve this goal? Do we have the resources we need? If not, how can we get them?

This question also applies to basic communication. Know what you want or what you're going to say, so you can state it clearly. Anticipate questions that might be asked about your statement or request.

Where are you right now?

In addition to identifying what we're trying to do, we also need to pay attention to our start point. As an example, if we're developing a plan for teaching a group of people something new, it's crucial to determine how much they already know. That's the start point for our audience, and it determines where the plan begins.

This question can be useful when we find ourselves in a bad situation. We can lose valuable time if we engage in pointless fantasizing about how much better off we'd be if we (or someone else) hadn't made the mistake that put us here.

We are where we are, not where we might have been. We fix the problem starting from that spot, not from where we'd like to be. Once we've gotten ourselves out of that situation, it may be helpful to revisit whatever put us there so we can avoid it in the future. Until we've resolved the issue, however, that discussion is wasted effort that needs to be applied to getting us out of the bad spot in which we've found ourselves.

All of this leads us to a key skill that many of us apply on a daily basis: Problem solving.

Basic problem solving

Learning to solve problems can pay off in a lot of ways. It can help you build self-confidence, sharpen your mind, and avoid procrastination. It increases your willingness to embrace challenges, because you're better able to deal with them.

The approach we're going to discuss can be applied to anything that needs a solution. So when we use the word *problem*, it can mean an undesirable set of circumstances such as getting stuck in traffic, or a challenging task such as deciding how to approach a long-term project.

When we use the word *solution*, we mean a decision or action that resolves the issue as completely as possible. Solutions are sometimes confused with answers, but the two terms are not interchangeable. All solutions are answers, but not all answers are solutions.

Say you're dealing with an overflowing toilet. Shutting off the water answers the immediate issue of spillage, but doesn't solve the overall problem of the malfunctioning toilet. Determining just what caused it to overflow, and then fixing that, is the solution.

Problem solving approach

Problem solving and decision making are related topics. Although not everything you encounter will be a problem, making good decisions ofetn involves some of the same analysis.

There are many approaches to problem solving. Here's one of them, in six steps:

1. Gather relevant information

2. Identify the problem

3. Decide what success looks like

4. Develop courses of action

5. Evaluate the courses of action

6. Choose an option

We'll be discussing this entire process, and then each of the steps, in the following pages. There's also a detailed example after that.

The importance of problem solving

Why should we learn how to find solutions to problems?

First, you may find yourself in a situation where you have no other choice. If the car you're driving has broken down in a desolate area and you forgot your phone, it helps to already have some idea how to get started resolving this predicament.

Second, in much of our modern world, problem solving has been replaced by denial, procrastination, and finger-pointing. Many people, some of them in positions of great responsibility, choose to ignore issues rather than fix them because solving the problem might force them to make unpopular decisions. The term "kicking the can down the road" sums this up well, because instead of fixing what's broken too many people pass it on to someone else.

Ignoring a problem doesn't make it go away. Kicking the can down the road not only postpones a job that needs to be done, but often turns it into a bigger job.

If you embrace problem solving, you'll gain good skills for improving bad situations.

Problem solving by steps

Why use this particular approach?

As long as you're dedicated to resolving the issue at hand, you should feel comfortable choosing any reliable method you like.

The approach we're going to explore here is a simple, straightforward method that has proven successful in the past. Although it contains vital steps such as correctly and fully identifying the problem at hand, it's offered here as one way among many to address a problem.

With that said, using a checklist/step-by-step approach can be quite helpful even outside of problem solving. It organizes the work to be done, specifies the tasks, and helps us to avoid overlooking a key action.

1. Gather relevant information

Whether we're making an important decision, organizing a job we're going to do, or attempting to solve an actual problem, chances are we already have some knowledge about the issue under discussion.

The more information we can collect about this topic, the better we'll be able to understand it. If you've ever had to stop working on a job and start over again with a different approach because you missed a key consideration when making the original plan, you know why it's so important to fully grasp the situation before getting started.

The results of this first step will influence all the others that follow, so be as complete as you can.

2. Identify the problem

This step is the most important of all. Have you ever been assigned a task, started work on that task, and then been told to stop doing it entirely? It's a frustrating experience that wastes time, and often means the planners incorrectly identified what was wrong or what needed to be done.

Take the time to fully identify the problem and its scope. It is highly unlikely that we will successfully resolve an issue if we don't know exactly what it is, don't determine what's causing it, or underestimate its size.

When we understand a problem, we position ourselves to develop a solution that fixes it. When we correctly assess the complete dimensions of an issue, we're reducing the chance we'll allocate insufficient resources as well.

On a related note, it's important not to *overestimate* the size of a problem. Some planners will exaggerate the scope of a project in order to impress someone or gain more authority. By doing this, they bring tasks into the mix that are unrelated to resolving the issue. Work hard to correctly identify the problem, its characteristics, and its true size so you can accurately develop a real solution.

3. Decide what success looks like

Before we can start developing potential approaches for solving the problem, we have to know what it means to successfully resolve the issue. In this step we are setting the standards, or criteria, for that success. We'll use those standards to help us develop potential options, to evaluate the probable effectiveness of those possible courses of action, and to select the one we will use.

This sounds obvious, but historically it's one of the most common stumbling blocks. Identifying the problem is the most important step, but establishing the conditions for its solution can be quite challenging.

If no clear conditions for success have been determined, it is impossible to know when we've solved the problem—if we solve it at all. The criteria for success will be used to help us develop our potential courses of action in Step 4 and then assess the likely effectiveness of those options in Step 5.

In short, you won't know when or if you've reached your destination if you don't know what that place looks like before you set out. You might go right by it, you might stop short, or you might end up some place very far away from where you intended.

4. Develop courses of action

Once we've reached this step, we've already determined the nature and scope of the problem and identified the conditions for success in its resolution.

Our initial collection of information also comes into play here, because we're brainstorming possible approaches or potential courses of action. By completing this step, we're also developing the basic outline of the plan we'll follow to solve the problem.

Take the time to create different approaches, because that thought process can help you make sure you're addressing all of the conditions for success. There is a temptation to stop brainstorming once we've come up with a course of action that seems appropriate to solving the problem.

Additionally, make sure the courses of action developed are within the range of you or your team's abilities—in other words, are they *achievable*? If they're not, can they be accomplished with extra help or additional resources?

In the next step you'll be evaluating each of these options, and if a disqualifying flaw is discovered in one of them it helps to have others.

5. Evaluate the courses of action

Fortunately, you've already done most of the hard work before you reach this step. You've created the options that you will now assess, and you've identified the standards those potential approaches must meet.

You are also going to be comparing the separate courses of action to each other. They might all meet the standards for success, but it's unlikely they'll all meet them in the same way.

Go through each potential course of action from start to finish, making sure every task it contains is something you can do, or taking note of what extra help you may need for that task.

You may discover that one or more courses of action won't satisfy the requirements for successful resolution of the issue. It's all right to drop that option at that time, but if this leaves you with only one course of action you should probably go back to Step 4 and generate a few more.

6. Choose an option

This step is the end result of all the others. By the time you're done evaluating the courses of action, you should know which one is the best.

You may have modified one of the options with parts of others, and you may have combined two course of action into one. If you've followed the steps, you are likely to have the outline of a workable plan that can now be filled in with details and specific tasks.

The reality of the actual work is unlikely to directly match the theory of our planning. Unanticipated obstacles will pop up, tasks will sometimes take longer than expected, and resources may not arrive on schedule.

If the plan is sound, these difficulties will become mere bumps in the road on the way to the successful arrival at our destination. You will still have to deal with them, but if you've developed an achievable plan that solves the problem, you'll reach the goal.

Problem solving example

You're driving a car down a highway where there aren't many houses or other cars. You stop at a rest area that has a restroom but no staff, and no one else is there.

Walking back to your car, you drop the key ring. The fob you need to unlock the car's doors and start the engine is on it. Unfortunately, the key ring falls onto a storm drain grate with holes just large enough to let it fall through, which it does.

Your phone is locked inside your car. You can't unlock the car or start the engine or drive away as things stand right now.

You have a real predicament on your hands, but if you've already learned how to address problems you'll be better equipped to handle this situation.

Let's go through the process now, beginning with Step 1: Gather relevant information.

1. Gather relevant information

You start by taking a look at your circumstances. The last house you saw was several miles back. There may be a closer house up the highway, but you haven't traveled that way yet and can't know for sure. Either way you'd have to walk.

You haven't seen many cars on the road. One might pull into the rest area, but so far nothing suggests that's likely to happen anytime soon.

There is no emergency phone in the restroom, but there is a mop with a removable handle you could use to reach into the storm drain. You also found a wire hanger you could twist into a hook. If you attached that to the mop handle, you might use it for snagging the key ring.

You can see your keys through the grate. They're three feet down, resting on a flat surface of dry dirt.

You're already coming up with different possible actions to take, but first you have to make sure they'll solve your problem. To do that, you have to correctly identify the problem itself. That's Step 2, and let's go into it now.

2. Identify the problem

What is the real problem here?

It's not the phone locked in the car. If the phone was in your pocket, you could call for help—but that wouldn't solve your problem. It would call someone who would still have to help you resolve the issue.

It's not even the key ring in the storm drain. That's close, but it's not the problem. It's the cause.

Here's your real problem: You can't currently operate the vehicle. You have to have the fob to open the car, start its engine, and drive away.

Still believe the problem is the keys in the storm drain? What if the fob got damaged in the drop? Even if you retrieve them, you'll still need a replacement fob to operate the car.

A true solution resolves the predicament. Whether you somehow get the key ring out of the storm drain, or get to a phone that you use to call for help, your issue isn't addressed until you're able to operate the car again.

This discussion right here is why this step is so important.

3. Decide what success looks like

Step 3 requires us to establish criteria for developing and evaluating proposed solutions.

In this example, any course of action we consider has to satisfy this question: Does this allow me to operate the car again?

To be even more specific, to operate the car you need to have a functioning fob in your possession that lets you unlock the car and drive away.

These are the bare minimum requirements for success. Any option you develop that doesn't meet those standards has to be rejected.

Let's consider other potential criteria that are important but not vital. Are you in a hurry? Do you feel safe where you are? How long can you wait there?

Two secondary criteria suggest themselves here: Speed and certainty. When you've developed your courses of action, you decide to include these two standards to help assess them. An option that takes less time is preferable, and any option that depends on chance is not.

4. Develop courses of action

In this step, it's common to formulate a single option that appears to be stronger than the others.

Don't stop once you've crafter that one course of action that you believe you'll end up choosing. Take the time to explore other options, because the obvious choice isn't always the most effective or efficient.

In this example, you're trying to get a functioning fob in your hand that works with the car you're driving. If the one in the storm drain still works, getting that out of the storm drain will meet those criteria. That's course of action (COA) 1.

What else might you do, especially if you can't find a way to retrieve the dropped fob? Remember the phone locked in the car. As much as you'd hate to do it, breaking one window would get you that phone. You could call for help to retrieve the dropped fob and, if it's broken, to get a replacement. That would meet the criteria for success, although it could take a long time. That's COA 2.

To avoid breaking the window, you might decide to simply wait and see if someone drives into the rest area. They may let you use their phone to call for help. It relies a lot on chance, but let's call it COA 3.

5. Evaluate the courses of action

Let's apply our four criteria to each COA to see how they measure up.

COA 1 will put a functioning fob in your hand if the one you dropped wasn't damaged. It won't take much time, and doesn't rely on chance. This COA meets all of the standards if the fob still works.

COA 2 gets you a phone at the cost of a broken window. Once help arrives, they may be able to snag your fob from the storm drain. If the fob doesn't work, they may be able to put you in touch with someone who can help you get a matching replacement. This COA takes a lot more time, because you'll have to wait for help and wait again if a replacement fob is needed. With that said, if the fob retrieved in COA 1 doesn't work you may have to switch to COA 2.

COA 3 only gets you help if someone drives into the rest area. So far you've seen no indication that this will happen. You could modify this COA so you go out to the road and try to flag someone down, but that's dangerous, takes time, and still relies a lot on chance.

6. Choose an option

Here's how our example shows us why it's so important to develop multiple COA's.

COA 1 meets all of the criteria better than the other two options—unless the fob is broken. If we'd only crafted COA 1 and then retrieved the broken fob, we would have been forced to start over.

The time consideration in COA 2 is important here. If the dropped fob is still working, COA 1 is likely to be the fastest solution. If the fob is damaged, COA 1 can end up costing time that is added onto COA 2 or COA 3.

We can't assume the fob is broken. Judging from where it landed, it probably isn't. So COA 1 will be chosen as the first solution attempted. If the fob no longer works, we'll immediately go to COA 2 because it takes less time and is less subject to chance than COA 3.

And if the phone we retrieve after breaking the window doesn't work for whatever reason, we'll go to COA 3.

Conclusion

Following this process sounds like an awful lot of effort, when your first inclination was to snag the key ring out of the storm drain. Right?

That is right. This example was designed to present the reader with a problem that isn't terribly complex. That way, the focus is on the steps and not the hypothetical problem.

If you get comfortable with this process, you'll know which steps you've already solved before you reach them. More important, you'll gain skills in key components of problem solving such as identifying the problem and developing realistic courses of action.

This process can also be applied to situations that aren't actual problems. It can help you explore approaches to difficult decisions, or plan how to tackle a challenging task or project.

Seeking Authenticity

We are the sum of our parts

As humans, we are complex beings. We're composed of many elements, which combine to make up the individual.

We are not just our good qualities, but also our bad ones. We aren't just our failures, but our successes too. We are everything we've done for others, and also the things we failed to do for them.

Ignoring any parts of ourselves that we don't particularly like doesn't make them go away or reduce their influence. Every one of our experiences, the good and the bad, holds a lesson.

It is highly beneficial to accurately see the different parts that make us a complete whole. If we can do that, we can gain a better understanding of ourselves and why we do the things we do. That deeper understanding can help us lead more authentic lives.

This also makes it easier for us to acknowledge our faults and own our mistakes. That in turn helps us to identify wrong or harmful behaviors we should discontinue. We may need some assistance in this effort, but if we honestly want to make a change, it is in our power to do so.

Standards

For our purposes, the word *standard* refers to a minimum level of quality or performance.

As an example for a minimum level of quality, when we buy a new piece of clothing we don't expect it to wear out the first time we put it in a washing machine.

Regarding a minimum level of performance, you probably already have standards for yourself and others. If you're an athlete, you may have a personal rule that you won't end a practice until you perform a key drill correctly ten times in a row. If you work in retail, you may have a personal standard that requires you to inspect every item being purchased to make sure it has no obvious flaws.

We may not always achieve these performance goals. If the bus is late, you may not be able to follow your rule about always getting to work on time.

With that said, personal standards represent our values and we don't easily let them slip. This is important for living an authentic life, because adhering to our values in adversity demonstrates something known as character.

Character

When we say someone has character, we're indicating that individual has ethical integrity or fortitude. In other words, they will maintain their standards in the face of opposition or difficulty.

Character is demonstrated when we do the right thing, or maintain a standard, when no one is watching or is likely to notice. When you have character, you hold yourself accountable to yourself.

This state of being is easily described, but not easily lived. As flawed individuals, we fall short of our ideals time and again. Those failures do not mean the standard was wrong or unimportant; it just means we didn't meet it that time. Character also teaches us to admit it when we come up short, to learn from that, and then try to do better in the future.

When you have character, your behavior becomes less dependent on circumstances and the influences of others. It's a form of independence, and as long as you genuinely believe in the standards you follow, it can help you lead an authentic life.

Motivations are unique

Every individual is unique, and each of us has a distinct set of motivations. There is certainly overlap, but no two people have the same motivations working on them with the same intensity and in the same way.

Motivations come in a wide range. People are prompted to behave the way they do by love, hate, altruism, greed, resentment, sympathy, self-aggrandizement, self-denial, and even apathy, just to name a few.

Why is it important to examine this? Because it highlights the difficulty we humans have in cooperating with each other and trusting each other. Too often entire groups of people are assumed to have identical goals and drives when every individual has a unique set of motivations. Beware of overgeneralizations and simple labels.

If each of us wants to choose the life we lead, then we shouldn't be surprised that others feel the same way. How they go about that will be strongly influenced by their motivations, and it's important to take that into account.

Don't follow the crowd

Let's discuss a strong motivation that can lead us down the wrong path. It combines our fear of embarrassment with a survival instinct called "strength in numbers" and is more commonly known as following the crowd.

When we don't follow the crowd, we can find ourselves standing alone. This can be an uncomfortable position. If we ultimately find out we're mistaken, we will be wrong and can look pretty foolish.

Resist this fear. Strive for accuracy, not popular approval. A false conclusion is still false—sometimes harmfully so—even if many people support it. Remember the times in history when the prevailing wisdom was wrong, such as the ardently defended belief long ago that the sun revolved around the earth.

There are people who'd rather be wrong standing with the crowd than be right standing alone. They can be critical, and even hostile, toward people who don't conform.

Remember, sometimes the "majority" is a small number of loud people with ulterior motives, and the "prevailing wisdom" is sometimes an ad campaign.

Consult multiple sources

No matter how we gain knowledge, there is always the danger that we're receiving bad information, drawing inaccurate or incomplete conclusions, or just arriving at the wrong answer.

The "world is a classroom" approach is a first step, but it isn't meant to be the only way we learn. First, it gives you a limited amount of information because it's guided by what you see and hear. Second, it's gathered through the prism of your viewpoint and may lack the perspective that a wider focus can provide.

To avoid that, treat the "world is a classroom" approach as just one method for gaining knowledge and wisdom. If you choose other sources such as formal education, reading, watching instructional or documentary media, performing new tasks you'd like to learn, and associating with reliable people who know more about a given topic than you do, you'll improve your chances of reaching better conclusions.

Consult multiple sources whenever you can. Check what you think you know.

Question your sources

Do you know people who offer advice that's usually bad, or who spout off on subjects about which they know very little? Do you take advice from them, or blindly repeat the information they provide without checking it?

Of course not. Your personal experience has shown you that their recommendations often lead to bad results and the input they offer is frequently wrong.

No one is perfect. We human beings all share at least one common denominator, in that we all have the capacity to be wrong. Even people who normally show good sense can make grievously bad decisions, and people who can usually be expected to provide good information can be mistaken sometimes.

This is another sound reason to consult multiple sources when possible. Use them to check what you're hearing and what you've already learned. In your own thinking, periodically take the time to question your assumptions and your conclusions.

You're making decisions based on the information you take in and what you've already learned. Make sure the information is sound and that your judgement is too.

Inconsistency as a measurement

We already mentioned the benefits of keeping your eyes and ears open. Now let's add something to that. Try to keep what you've seen and heard in your memory. Pay attention to how the people in your life and work behave. If that behavior changes, there's often a reason. Hopefully it's a positive reason, but in any event you're seeing an inconsistency.

When something is inconsistent, it doesn't match or fit what came before it. It's beneficial to notice inconsistency wherever you find it—especially when dealing with other people. Do their deeds match their words? Do the words they're speaking to one audience match what they say to a different audience? Does their behavior under one set of circumstances match their behavior under others?

Inconsistency can also help you analyze subjects beyond behavior. The performance of a machine. The validity of a theory. The soundness of a suggestion. Is what you hear and see consistent, or does something stand out?

Sometimes it's not what you see, but what you don't. What would you expect to see under a given set of circumstances? Are you seeing that? If not, why not?

.

Inconsistency example

Here's an example. Some people will attempt to convince you to stop using something that works, just because it's been around for a while.

There's an apt saying on this topic: Make sure the new bucket doesn't leak before you throw out the old one.

The world is full of people selling leaky buckets, and they can be convincing. They'll tell you it's a better material that's lighter and stronger. If there's money in it, they're likely to tell you anything.

Look for the inconsistencies. Examine their argument to see if it logically proves their recommendation.

Does it matter that the new bucket is stronger, assuming that's true? The old one has worked well for years, so it's strong enough. Does it matter that the new bucket, when empty, is lighter than the old one? When either bucket is full of water, the weight of the water is what makes it heavy—and that's the same in both buckets.

Our world is full of trickery. Now let's discuss ways to identify that and deal with it.

Recognizing Duplicity

Communication

There are two reasons we communicate with each other: To give something, or to get something.

That isn't as sinister as it sounds. Most communications fall into two categories: We're either giving information or getting information.

At other times we're asking people to perform a task or they're asking us.

Good communication is vital to interactions. It can lead to greater transparency and fuller understanding—both of which can lead to improved relationships.

Unfortunately, bad communication abounds. Much of this is unintentional. Try as we may, language isn't a perfect medium for thought and we are often misunderstood or don't understand what was said to us.

Bad communication can be intentional too. Words can be used to deceive, confound, and manipulate. It's important to be aware of this and recognize when it happens.

Let's look at that now.

Emotion vs. logic

Some people don't want you to have the chance to think things over (for example, a bad business proposition or a flawed argument) because they fear you'll see what's wrong. Thought, and the time to apply it, is their enemy. To prevent that, they may try to rush you, distract you, or cloud your judgment.

Emotion can provoke a response that then blocks careful consideration. People trying to deceive you may couch their approach in a way that elicits a reaction that either gets you to do what they want or keeps you from thinking.

People who know their arguments won't stand up under scrutiny may try to prevent that analysis through carefully worded jabs. "This isn't something you need to be afraid of" and "Change can be unsettling" are two phrases that sound reasonable but suggest you lack courage or are too set in your ways. They're meant to make you angry or resentful. They're also designed to make anyone who's listening suspect your opposition comes from an inability to adapt to what is being presented as a great new idea.

This deceptive behavior is intended to prevent rational examination and genuine discussion.

Emotion as manipulation

Manipulation is deceptive persuasion. Manipulation gets people to do something they aren't likely to do if given the opportunity to think. Appeals to emotion are some of the easiest methods of manipulation because strong emotions can cloud our minds while also getting us to act. Both positive and negative emotions can be used in this way.

The Roman gladiators had a saying: Anger is death. This was a reminder that opponents would try to annoy them in combat, to get them to act impulsively. Acting based on emotion is the opposite of acting based on reason, and this tactic was designed to goad them into attacking wildly, forgetting their training and making them easier to defeat.

Think of all the harm that has been done by appeals to emotion that were meant to inflame passions and remove reason. Holy wars and vendettas. False rumors that set neighbors, friends, and coworkers against each other. Propaganda meant to dehumanize an opponent and justify unacceptable acts.

Be aware of this form of deceptive persuasion. Watch out for arguments, stories, and images designed to elicit an emotional response. Is this manipulation?

Why we shouldn't tell lies

Authentic things are genuine, which means they are not false. Lies are false. It is very difficult to live an authentic life if we say things that are false.

Truth is reality and lies are fantasy. When we tell a lie, we have to remember its specifics because the lie disagrees with the facts. That's one way that telling lies separates us from reality. We have to "stick to our story" and try to make it match up with related facts and explain why it doesn't seem to make sense. The more we do this, the weaker our grip on reality can become.

This isn't a reference to minor departures from the truth such as saying a friend's new haircut looks fine when it doesn't. No, the lies we're discussing are the kind that mislead others. They can cost people money or reputation or their peace of mind—and they're usually intended to do just that.

The impulse to lie can be an emotional defense response when we fear the consequences of telling the truth. Remember the discussion of emotion versus reason, and don't give in to this. Make yourself apply reason and you may avoid the impulse to lie—and all of the problems that come with sticking to a lie.

Lies and trust

There are real consequences to lying.

Lies are a betrayal of trust because they mislead others. When people find out we deceived them, their belief in us is damaged and may never be regained. They have reason to distrust us going forward, and to warn others about us.

There is a popular misconception about the acceptability of lying in business relationships. While concepts such as *caveat emptor* and *laissez-faire* are often heard as excuses for business deceptions, nobody enjoys being cheated. In cases of fraud, money or value is actually lost. Victims of that kind of deception feel like they helped someone rob them, and so their response isn't likely to be tolerant.

Many business deals involve trust. Credit is extended and orders are placed, just to name two common "good faith" arrangements. If that faith is broken, the individuals or businesses at fault can find themselves losing suppliers and customers. They can be required to obey strict rules regarding payment or performance, such as money-in-front or cash-on-delivery, and because they lied they have no choice but to comply.

Don't play your adversary's game

It's fitting to refer to someone who's trying to trick you as an adversary. While you may have joined a discussion expecting logic and reason, once you realize that deceitful tactics are being employed, you now have an adversary.

Negotiation and argument are a part of life. If you find yourself in a discussion with someone who's trying to deceive you, isn't allowing you to speak, or is obviously taking you through a preplanned argument, don't play their game. Their game is designed to make them the winners, so it's not a good idea to go along with it.

One technique to avoid getting taken through someone else's devious playbook is to ask questions that are related to the topic but not their argument. They're not dealing with you honestly, so it's a perfectly acceptable ploy. Ask an unexpected question on a point of order or explanation of a term, and you'll appear completely reasonable while also requiring your adversary to respond.

Disrupt your adversary's planned attack, and you'll buy the time to apply logic that they're trying to deny you.

See through the smokescreen

Someone who wants to convince you to do something that's not in your best interest may try to blur your sense of reality. That's not surprising, if they want something bad to appear to be something good.

Some arguments can sound like they make perfect sense even when you know what they're recommending has failed in the past. Insist on being granted the time to think these arguments through, especially if you're being urged to take quick action.

Follow the logic from its start point to its stated goal or result. Does the argument stay consistent and logical the whole way? Is the recommended action likely to achieve the goal, or at least move toward it?

Even if the answers are yes, that doesn't mean this is the *best* option to adopt. Are there more effective or efficient ways of accomplishing the same goal? If so, why would someone be recommending a less efficient, less effective method?

Consider their motivations. Ask how this recommended action benefits them beyond the obvious.

Debate calmly

If you're in a debate or even a full-blown argument, try to maintain a calm demeanor. This isn't fakery, because it represents the polite discussion you'd prefer to be having.

Just thinking about presenting a calm appearance can help lower your agitation. We often demonstrate our natural reactions to what others are saying through our facial expressions and tone of voice. It's natural to respond to competition or conflict with excitement, unease, and even fear. The trick is to not show it.

Remember what we discussed about emotion being the opposite of reason? You need to be thinking straight to make your argument. So strive to control your reactions to your adversary's insults or whatever else they might try.

You may also have an audience, so appearing calm and composed can help to win them over or convince them to listen to your argument. People generally don't respond well to someone who's angry or flustered. Project a cool confidence, and they will at least hear you out.

The indirect approach

Sometimes we encounter people who won't cooperate no matter what we do. Ever try to work with people who clearly weren't interested in doing their jobs?

If they're being paid to assist you and you haven't been rude, they're actually choosing not to cooperate. Repeated requests or threats to complain aren't likely to move them.

Unless you have recourse to someone who can make them cooperate, you may have to adopt an indirect approach. Taking them head-on isn't going to work, so look for a strategy that will.

Start by reversing the process. Instead of building a plan based on the current impasse, build it backward from the desired outcome. Imagine the individuals doing what you asked, and then brainstorm any factors and influences that might motivate them to do that.

Is there someone they respect who could intervene? Do they have a rival you could approach for the same thing, prompting them to act to keep from being embarrassed? Brainstorm motivations for them to do their jobs, and then ask yourself how to apply those motivations.

Navigating the world

Attitude influences everything

For our purposes, an attitude is our mental disposition toward something or someone.

Our attitudes influence our behavior. As an example, if we have a negative attitude toward someone, we probably won't be eager to work with that person if asked. If we have a receptive attitude toward new experiences, we're likely to accept invitations to go places we've never been before.

Attitudes can be learned. The hostile disposition from the first example probably didn't come out of thin air; the negative reaction toward that individual is likely to have been prompted by an earlier bad experience.

Because attitude is so closely linked to behavior, it often has a direct impact on results. A defeatist attitude expects failure, and can cause us to not put forth a good effort. A selfless attitude places the needs of others ahead of our own, and lets us approach a task with greater objectivity.

Attitudes can be shaped. Build confidence in your ability to solve problems and make decisions, and your response to challenging situations will be more positive.

See the good with the bad

When things aren't going well, it's natural to focus on what's wrong. There's a value to recognizing these wrong things, because we can't fix what we don't see. However, it's equally important, in good times and bad, to recognize the things that are going well.

What puts a smile on your face? What went right today, or yesterday, or recently? Who do you look forward to seeing, or what do you look forward to doing? What in your immediate vicinity is a thing of beauty you haven't noticed?

Stop and look at the sky every now and then, in daytime and nighttime. Appreciate the clouds and the stars. See the trees and the bushes and the vines and the grass you pass by every day.

These sights exist without your involvement. Recognizing these things can help us to gain perspective on our lives, our troubles, and the world in general. Perspective can help us manage stress and decide how we view our surroundings and even our existences.

Limit the negativity in your life

Negativity is any influence that lowers your optimism or wastes your time. Both instances can seriously impact your mental well-being, your ability to function, and your overall attitude. You have a right to limit those effects.

This doesn't mean you have to shut them out entirely. Some of these influences are friends and relatives, and others can't be completely avoided. The point is to control your exposure to them so that they don't subtract from your well-being so much.

Regarding negative people, identify what they're doing that's affecting you. If possible, discuss this with them. If that's not possible, create a plan for limiting how much you're exposed to this influence. If someone calls you frequently and then spends the entire call complaining, say at the outset that you can only talk for X minutes and then stick to that.

Some negative influences subtract from our time. They make us feel agitated because we know we could be doing something else. Examine how your time is being wasted and why you're involved in that activity, and see if there is any way to reduce that effect or avoid being put in that position so often.

The role of perception

How we see our personal situations and surroundings influences our attitudes and behaviors. Our perceptions impact our ability to deal with those circumstances—both positively and negatively. Focus only on what's wrong or what's hindering you, and you're likely to develop a pessimistic view of your ability to improve the situation.

This doesn't mean we should ignore problems or pretend an obstacle is less formidable than it is. False perceptions, both good and bad, are misleading. We need to assess our surroundings—our *entire* surroundings—as they are.

A good first step is to make sure we see ourselves, our environments, and our challenges clearly and accurately. No matter how tough a situation might appear to be, just demonstrating the mental strength to recognize it is a way to control its effect on us.

When we do this, we're refusing to deny reality or shy away from difficulty. If we add our experiences with problem solving and our competence with the other applicable skills to this perspective, our confidence levels will rise accordingly. By adopting this attitude, we may find we no longer feel the need to see things except as they truly are.

Find a place to think

Our modern world is filled with distractions. We spend every day surrounded by people and devices that are fighting to gain and hold our attention.

Many of us have become so used to this environment that we're uncomfortable with silence and tranquility.

Unfortunately, it's very difficult to concentrate in a space that's filled with noise and activity. While most of us can perform simple or familiar tasks in those circumstances, our attention is divided and our ability to think deeply is reduced.

If you have to give serious thought to a weighty issue, it's helpful to create the right environment.

To do this, find a place where the noise level is low and there isn't much going on. You should feel comfortable and relaxed in that spot. Shut off your phone, and be still for a few minutes.

Try not to think of anything at all at first, so your mind can calm itself. Then consider the problem or issue at hand. You will find this much easier without distractions, and your thinking will be much more effective.

Meditation

Giving your mind a break from noise and distractions can help you make a big decision. Giving your mind a break from itself can be even more beneficial.

Our minds are always working. Like every worker, they need rest. Meditation can give your mind that rest. The basic concept is to shift our awareness from your thoughts to a simple task or process.

Here's one basic meditation method you can try. Find a safe spot that's free of distractions. You can shut your eyes or keep them open. Focus your attention on your breathing by inhaling slowly for five seconds and then exhaling slowly for five seconds. Work on filling your lungs deeply with each inhale, and emptying them with each exhale. Concentrate on each successive breath.

Thoughts will still come into your mind. Acknowledge them, but then return your focus to your breathing. Do this for just a few minutes at first, and see if you feel calmer afterward.

There are countless ways of doing this, so if this interests you, consider exploring different forms of meditation to find the one that works best for you.

Examine failures and successes

It makes sense to review things that didn't go the way we hoped. It can be an uncomfortable process, but to avoid that experience in the future we need to understand how it went wrong.

Don't wallow in every mistake and missed opportunity. You've already experienced the negative effects of those errors, so now get the positive ones. Go through every step of the job or task that didn't work out so you don't miss anything. It's easy to overlook an important learning point while focusing on the biggest error of the bunch.

Examine our successes? Why would we need to do that?

Because sometimes things go well when they shouldn't have. Successes can really boost our confidence, but if all we do is celebrate them we may miss valuable insights. We may also gain a false idea of our abilities, or overlook one aspect that needs improvement. Look closely at what worked.

If you discover that your planning and execution were the reason for this achievement, so much the better. Now see if that approach can be used on other tasks or projects.

Competence builds confidence

Once you gain skills and experience in problem solving, you may also start feeling better about yourself and the future. That's because you're proving concretely that you can positively impact things that impact you. You also gain confidence in your ability to navigate your future, because you've successfully handled challenging tasks and difficult situations in the past.

We're all human and we're all flawed. We have all failed somewhere, and we have all let other people down. Other people have let us down too—sometimes intentionally.

By more gaining skills and confidence, you better equip yourself to deal with those times when things don't work out and people don't come through for you.

The more you can do, the less you're dependent on others and on circumstances. The more you can do, the better you'll understand the world around you. The more you can do, the better trained your mind will be to analyze situations and envision ways to improve or fix them.

Plan ahead

Just about anything we rely on can abruptly disappear.

Ask yourself what would happen if something you need wasn't available anymore? What would you do to replace it, or how would you adapt to living without it? What can you do to be better prepared if that actually does happen?

This is another benefit of continuously developing your mind and gaining new skills. If you have to learn how to perform a task because whoever usually does that isn't available right now, your earlier experiences expanding your capabilities will help you get organized. They'll also reassure you that you can master something unfamiliar.

It's better not to be put in that position in the first place, however. By reviewing those things on which we depend, we can imagine how difficult it might be to do them for ourselves or do without them. That analysis tells us which items or services would pose the greatest problem if they disappeared, and from there we can start planning what we'd do in their absence.

Plan ahead for developments that could seriously impact you, and then decide how you'd deal with them.

Keep things organized

Does any of the following sound familiar? It's tax time, and you spend days trying to find last year's return and the receipts you need.

Life is complicated enough, so it's a good idea to keep important things organized. It doesn't have to be fancy. For your taxes, designate a drawer or a shoebox as the spot where you collect all those documents you end up searching for at filing time. As each one arrives during the year, put it in there.

What else do you have a hard time finding when you need it? The remote for the television? Your keys? Set up a tray or a bowl as their resting spot, and make yourself put them there every time you set them down.

If you make this a habit, it may give you a subconscious boost. Too much low-level disorder can make us think our entire lives are out of control—but managing that disorder can give us the opposite feeling.

Don't believe it? Take some time to go through wherever you live and put all those things away that you set down "just for now" weeks or months ago. Neaten the place up, and then notice how much better this made you feel.

Money is a tool

Money is described as a "medium of exchange" because we use it to facilitate business transactions like buying and selling. Before money, we had other systems such as barter that were more difficult to use. Money is nothing more than a tool that makes our lives easier.

Like most other tools, money is a good servant and a poor master. We direct what it does, not the other way around.

Money can get us many of the things we want. Goods. Services. Security. As long as we do nothing wrong or unethical to get it, we're still in control of it.

Money can influence some of our actions. For example, we might not be able to buy the exact item we want because it costs more than we have. In that case, money has caused us to buy the less expensive version.

Be careful about what you let money make you do. We all know cases where people lied, cheated, and stole in order to get money. If we do those things, we're treating others in a way that we wouldn't want to be treated, and we're letting a tool tell us what to do.

Managing money

It's difficult to focus on living our authentic lives when we're worried. One of the chief worries for many people is money, so let's talk about ways to address that.

This section offers basic techniques involving budgeting, spending, and saving. Everyone is different, so the tips that follow may not fit your situation exactly. Because your financial circumstances are unique, they require an approach designed specifically for you.

We'll also discuss ways to get sound advice on managing your money from people you know who've been in circumstances similar to yours. You should consider consulting reputable professionals before making any big decisions about your finances.

The following tips are some of the most fundamental approaches and considerations in budgeting. This segment includes recommendations about saving money for the future, but it also recognizes that putting money aside may not be possible for you at this time. This section is designed to demonstrate respect for your circumstances while also offering concrete advice that may be helpful both now and in the future.

Budgeting basics

For our discussion, a budget is a tool for coordinating your income and your expenses. It estimates how much money you bring in (your income) and how much money you use (your spending) in a given period. While we'll mostly be focused on your monthly income and spending, some important expenses (such as an annual excise tax) are less frequent but must also be considered.

By evaluating your income and your spending, you can gain a better understanding of how much you're making and how you're using it.

Here are some excellent sources for the information you'll need to construct your budget:

To calculate your total income, you can consult your tax returns, bank statements, pay records, and the records of any other sources of income you may have.

To examine your spending, you can consult your bank statements, credit card statements, and the records of any automatically recurring payments you may have.

Let's start with income.

Budgeting basics
How much are you bringing in?

Determining exactly how much income you have tells you how much new money is available in a given period. For simplicity, we'll be staying with monthly figures unless otherwise stated.

Your income can be separated into two varieties: Reliable and variable.

Reliable income is any recurring payment that is the same amount every time you receive it. For example, a monthly salary is often a fixed number.

Variable income involves recurring payments that are different each time you receive them. Examples are tips and overtime pay.

Now that we know the two kinds of income, let's look at spending.

How much money are you using?

Examining monthly spending can help you gain a better understanding of where your money goes.

Your spending (or expenses) can be separated into two varieties: Essential and discretionary.

Essential spending involves all those things we can't do without (such as food and electricity) and mandatory payments (such as the rent or mortgage) each month.

Discretionary spending involves the expenses that aren't absolutely necessary. Examples are the cost of going out to dinner or going on vacation. This shouldn't suggest that these expenses are frivolous or that you should eliminate them. You're allowed to have fun in your life.

 Now that we've got an understanding of the two kinds of income and the two kinds of spending, let's see how they relate to each other.

Income and spending

This exercise is a good example of basic analysis. Instead of viewing your monthly income as a total dollar amount, you're now aware of how much of that figure is fixed every month and how much of it can fluctuate.

Likewise, separating total spending into essential and discretionary expenses allows us to see which spending is mandatory and which is optional.

Obviously we'd like the total income to be larger than the total spending. Ideally, we'd like to see all the essential spending covered by the reliable income.

Unfortunately, sometimes that's not the case—and if our spending is consistently larger than our income, we need to look for a solution.

Increasing our incomes can be difficult or impossible, but reducing the spending number is an option sometimes. Let's look at that now.

Reducing spending

Let's revisit our two spending categories. We said that essential spending involves all those things we can't do without (such as food and electricity) and payments we have to make each month (such as the rent or mortgage).

Just because the expense is unavoidable doesn't mean we can't look at reducing it. We still have to buy food, but perhaps there's a less expensive version of what we're purchasing that's just as good. Even the payments we absolutely must make have the potential for reduction—we might consider finding an apartment with lower rent or perhaps getting a roommate.

Discretionary spending is easier to reduce. After all, these expenses aren't absolutely necessary. Reviewing each item in this category might provide good savings.

As stated earlier, that doesn't mean we have to eliminate all our non-essential spending. Life can be tough without fun and relaxation.

Budgeting basics
If money is left over

If we spend less money than we make, the question is what to do with the extra. The future is never certain, so putting that money away is a sensible option. We can save the money so it's available in an emergency, or we can invest it so it grows, or we can try to do both.

Unexpected expenses (such as a car repair) can seriously throw off a budget if we were making only a little more than we were spending. So one option for any extra money left over after monthly expenses is to set it aside as an *emergency fund*. Even small amounts quickly add up, and if we make sure we don't dip into that money it can eventually reach a level where it can pay for most of an unexpected expense.

Thinking long-term, another option for extra money is to invest it. By doing this, we're not just saving that money. We're putting it to work for us.

The mechanics of investment are too detailed to go into here, but now let's look at who you might consult about your budget, managing your money, and what to do with any money left over at the end of the month.

Budgeting basics
Talk to people who know

Remember the section on making sure we consult good sources of information? What we're going to discuss now is a great example of that.

We already mentioned that we might consider consulting a reputable financial professional, but how would we know which one is right for us? How would we know if we're ready for that step?

The answers are close by. Talk to friends, relatives, and coworkers you trust who are successfully managing their money. The key word there is *successfully*. It's probably not a good idea to consult the friend who is constantly bumming cash off everyone and not paying it back.

Do you know someone who has (or once had) a financial situation similar to yours? Older relatives can be excellent sources of advice, because many of them have been where you are now. Friends and coworkers facing the same financial challenges you are, but who are handling them well, are also good sources.

Talk to people who know. How did they balance their incomes and expenses? Did they consult a finance professional? If they did, how did they go about selecting that professional?

Interacting With Others

Practice situational awareness

This topic is exactly what it sounds like—but more. At its most basic, practicing situational awareness asks us to pay attention to our surroundings in terms of what's there, what's happening, and what might be developing.

In an earlier segment we discussed keeping our eyes and ears open as a means of learning from the world around us. This is very similar.

On an individual level, situational awareness assesses a locale and everything in it. It tells us where the exits are located, and that a stranger seems to be paying too much attention to what we're doing. On a more positive note, it tells us when our impromptu discussion is blocking traffic in a hallway and prompts us to move aside.

One you get into this habit, you may begin to anticipate developments around you even as they're happening.

Situational awareness can extend beyond your immediate environment. In business terms, if you keep track of your industry and the actions of your peers, you may notice when change is on the way—not when it arrives.

Practice being aware of what's going on around you.

Close the loop in all things

The term "closing the loop" refers to the conscientious management of communications and coordinations in an action or a project.

Have you ever been left wondering if someone else has performed a crucial task as assigned or agreed? Been unsure if an important message or package you sent was received? Become concerned that a final action in a long string of tasks hasn't been completed?

It's not a comfortable feeling, and it can be avoided if we commit to closing the loop in everything. Keep people updated. Reply to messages—even the ones where you don't yet have an answer—to let the senders know you received them and are working toward a resolution. When you've located the item for tomorrow's party that the event's organizer was searching for, let everyone know so they can all stop looking.

Once you start doing this, it may become a part of your planning. You'll start anticipating instances where you'd appreciate someone else closing the loop with you—and you'll ask them ahead of time to make sure they do.

Finally, if you say you're going to do something, do it.

Seeking attention

Some people do the right thing just to be seen doing it. They often discuss or publicize their actions, because they want and need the attention and praise.

This behavior is obvious. It practically screams, "Look at me!" and suggests we're not comfortable moving through the world without an audience.

When we try to attract attention for our positive acts, it takes away from the deed itself. Instead of seeing a kind gesture that might inspire them to do the same later, the witnesses to our good deed may only remember our self-publicity. Disgusted by this display of selfishness, they may question our motives and even portray our behavior as neediness and insecurity.

Do a good job for the satisfaction of a task well done or because the job needed doing. Do good deeds to benefit whomever was in need. If you also receive accolades for this, it's a nice reward that you didn't seek or expect. That makes it both genuine and deserved.

If your actions are dictated by who might be watching, they'll never be genuine—and neither will you.

The cost of laziness

The idea that inactivity has a cost may sound strange, but it's also true. When laziness causes us to put off a chore or task, it incurs the risk that the job we're not doing now will be harder to do later.

Scrubbing down the walls of a bathtub or a shower isn't a fun chore, but if we don't do it frequently, the long-term buildup we have to eventually remove can require much more effort.

Laziness goes beyond inactivity, though. It can apply to our thought processes too. "Lazy thinking" is at fault when we jump to an easy conclusion or fail to study every option. In the first case, the wrong conclusion can send us down a road going nowhere. In the second, we may believe we've puzzled through a problem only to discover we didn't ponder it nearly enough.

Laziness can also involve taking the easy way out of a tough job. Oddly, turning in less than satisfactory work frequently forces us to put in even more effort as a result. If what we did doesn't meet the standard, we'll probably have to do it over.

Commitment

Sadly, the world is full of people who take jobs without any intention of actually doing those jobs. Though willing to accept the pay and benefits, they refuse to take on the responsibilities.

This behavior can be found outside the employment realm as well. Some people will accept elected office, positions of high authority or trust, or even the role of relationship partner with no intention of doing any of the work that role demands.

This is deceitful behavior because in almost every case the individual applied for this role in some way. Promises were made, agreements were signed, or personal oaths were given—all while the individual never intended to fulfill the role's responsibilities.

This behavior robs anyone who had a right to expect the honoring of those promises, and it robs them twice. They not only experience the disappointment of the individual who took the job and didn't do it, but they also miss the chance to give the job to someone who cares.

Do the job, do it right, or let someone else do it.

Respect the power of example

While we shouldn't do things so that others will see them, we should still remember that people watch what we do.

We never know when our actions are being observed by someone who may be influenced by our behavior. Has anyone ever told you that you inspired them at some point in the past and you didn't know it at the time? Ever hear someone remark that a chance encounter with a stranger who demonstrated selflessness or kindness changed their attitude for the better? That's the power of good example.

One of the reasons good example is so effective is that it leaves no room for hypocrisy. You're not telling anyone how they should behave—your actions are inspiring them. Deeds not words.

It's important to remember the power of bad example too. We sometimes don't know who looks up to us, or who believes we have better answers than they do. If we do something wrong, or demonstrate selfishness or a lack of caring, we may be suggesting to that individual that our bad behavior is acceptable.

Setting the example

Have you ever been impressed by someone else's actions to the extent that you decided to imitate them?

Ever watched a stranger pick up some stray litter that was blowing around and toss it in a waste receptacle?

Been impressed by a coworker's meticulous attention to detail?

Heard a manager who was being praised for a great job say it was someone else's work, and that the author of that work should receive the accolades?

If you did, this was the power of good example in action. The people you observed all demonstrated a commitment to positive standards of behavior without saying a word about it. Setting the example might not have been their motivation, but they accomplished it just the same.

When we act in accordance with our values and standards, we can inspire others. There's a fine line between setting the example and doing something to attract attention, but if we do the same thing whether someone else is watching or not, it will be genuine.

The tipping point

A tipping point is the spot or moment when enough force or influence has been added to a situation or system to cause a dramatic change. A cat nudging a glass toward the edge of a table will finally move it to a place where one more nudge will send it over.

Tipping points apply to individuals, groups, governments, organizations, societies, markets, and many others.

There's a tipping point to success, and to failure.

When you've got more people doing something right than doing it wrong, it becomes more difficult to do it wrong because of example, peer pressure, and the inability to claim you didn't know better.

Unfortunately, the opposite is equally true. When you have more people doing something wrong than doing it right, it becomes much harder to do it right because of peer pressure, a sense of futility, and doubt.

Make the conscious choice to add your influence on the positive and productive side of the tipping point. One nudge, either way, can make the difference.

Managing a project

Projects come in all sizes and types, but you can use this approach with just about all of them.

If you're a manager of teams or individuals, or if you're just organizing volunteers who are working together, you can apply what follows.

There's an old three-word approach to managing projects that will get you started: Organize. Deputize. Supervise.

Organize: In this step, you'll use the problem-solving skills we discussed earlier to help develop a plan. As you choose your approach, consider what resources will be needed. Break the plan down into specific tasks, and then consider who or what is going to handle each of them.

Deputize: Assign tasks to the people or teams that will perform them. Let them take charge of whatever you gave them. Don't micromanage. Remember, the farther you are from where the work is being done, the less you will understand the conditions, circumstances, and obstacles.

Supervise: Ultimately, you're the one responsible for the completion of this project. Monitor the work, make sure each task meets its stated goal or standard, and ensure the people doing the work have the support they need.

Communicate accurately

This is a valuable idea in everyday life, but it's especially helpful in project management.

There are plenty of ways to be misunderstood in written and spoken communications. If we honestly don't know something for sure, it's better to indicate that clearly than to guess. If we don't have a specific number but know the amount isn't large, it's acceptable to say "some" or "a few". However, we should try to be as specific as possible whenever we can.

If a task is going to take between two and three days, we might be tempted to describe that as using "a few" days. While that is true, it's not as accurate as it could be. Instead, try saying "not less than two and not more than three" if you're sure about those numbers.

When we pay attention to communicating with accuracy, we notice those times when we were being unnecessarily vague. This can help to focus our attention on gaining specific information, which will in turn warn us when we don't have exact data and need it.

Communicating accurately is a great aid when assigning tasks to others. Let's look at that now.

What and why

When we give someone a task, it's important to explain its purpose. This is basic courtesy, and it shows that we recognize that individual might be able to provide useful suggestions if fully read in on the situation.

It can pay big dividends when circumstances change and the individual performing that task already understands its purpose.

Here's an example. You're managing a house remodeling crew. You tell a team member to wait for the delivery truck while you and the others go to the work site. The expected delivery is an emergency order of decorative nails that is holding up the job. If you don't explain what the delivery is and why it's important, that team member will bring you whatever the driver provides.

If you tell the team member what's being delivered, the shipment can be checked to make sure it's right. If you take the time to explain why the delivery is important, that team member may remember seeing an unused case of those nails left over from a previous job, saving you valuable time.

When people understand the purpose of a task, they can adapt more easily to unexpected changes and potentially make a stronger contribution.

Keeping track

Whether you're managing teams or individuals, workers or volunteers, it's important to have a system for keeping tabs on who's doing what and when they're doing it.

This tool also helps the people who are doing the work to see the larger picture and to plan ahead.

Create a tracking matrix: A matrix is an arrangement of squares or rectangles in rows and columns. For example, a monthly calendar is a matrix that lines up the days of a week in a single row and then stacks those weeklong rows on top of each other.

In a way, your tracking matrix will be like a calendar. The top row, going from left to right, will list all of the days and dates of your project, from start to finish.

The column farthest to the left will list every individual and team that has responsibilities in your project. Those names will be a stacked from top to bottom.

In each of the boxes in the matrix's body, you'll write the tasks to be completed—under the day they're being done and across from the name of whoever is doing them. If a task takes three days, three boxes side to side will show that task from start to finish. The days and dates in the top row tell everyone when the task begins and when it's due.

Getting started

Spreadsheet software is an excellent tool for creating tracking matrices. It's already formed into rows, and you can type information right into the boxes, or cells. You can also draw a matrix or use index cards on a board.

Let's say you're planning a party that will take place in two weeks, on a Saturday night. Begin your matrix by creating the top row. Leave the top left-most box empty, because that's the column showing the people doing the work and their names go under that.

In the next box over in the top row, enter the name of your first project workday and its date. Then enter all of the days and dates, going from left to right, until the Saturday of the party. This top row is your timeline.

Next, list everyone who will be helping with the party in the left-most column, vertically, one to each box. These might be the names of individuals, but perhaps they'll be the names of stores that have the full responsibility for a task—such as a florist that will deliver decorations.

You now have an empty matrix that shows your project timeline across the top, and everyone involved in the project down the far left side.

Fill in the specifics

Your planning has already identified the tasks that have to be accomplished. In most cases, it's also identified who's going to handle each of those tasks.

Find the name of whoever is responsible for a specific task in the left-hand column and then find the box in that row that matches the dates of that task in the timeline above. As an example, if your sister has volunteered to design and send out electronic invitations by Tuesday of the first week in the timeline, enter that deadline in the row with her name under the timeline box for that date.

Do the same thing for all of the tasks that have already been assigned. Take a moment to review the results. The tracking matrix is very helpful, because it shows all of this information in one spot. Does one volunteer have too many tasks? Is there a task that needs to be completed before another one begins, but the dates for those tasks don't agree? Are there any tasks that have been forgotten?

Remember the florist that will deliver the decorations? Is anyone assigned to confirm that, and when should they be making that call?

Using the matrix

Even with short-duration projects, check to see what else is going on at the same time.

Don't send out the invitations only to discover that your party is on the same day as a close relative's wedding. Don't build a detailed plan for the two weeks you think you have, only to notice that the weekend in the middle of your plan has a national holiday on Monday and many of your volunteers will have plans for that weekend.

Believe it or not, these things happen.

Depending on the size of your project, you may want to schedule interim meetings with the entire group or check-ins with individuals as part of supervising the whole process. When you enter those items on the matrix, ask yourself if there will be enough time to fix anything missed or misunderstood that you only discover at that meeting or in that phone call.

Finally, consider adding a day or two onto the timeline for cleanup and returning anything rented for the party. How big a job is that, and who's going to do it?

Ask "What if?"

So now we've built a plan showing all assigned tasks and the dates for their completion.

Plans don't always go according to plan. In every aspect of life, it's a good idea to ask "What if?" to imagine some possible, or even likely, ways the schedule could run into trouble.

You won't anticipate everything that can go wrong, so try to concentrate on the ones that are most probable.

Let's use a new example, a two-adult home with children where both adults work full-time away from the home. They already do project management on a daily basis. They're juggling schedules for work, daycare, school, and activities, just to name a few.

Let's assume they already did their "What if?" planning. So when a child at daycare becomes sick and has to go home, they know which one of the adults is going to handle that. They also know the backup plan, if that adult isn't able to go get the child for whatever reason.

Asking "What if?" helps us to imagine potential wrinkles in our plans and prepare for them ahead of time. It's well worth the effort.

<u>Heading Out</u>

Contemplate existence

This topic sounds a little heavy, doesn't it? Pondering the topic of existence is a big job, but what we've covered here has already positioned you to get started.

By now you've identified some behaviors you respect and some you don't. You may have selected some values upon which you'll rely as you go through life. Choices like those can form the foundation of your philosophy on the subject of life and existence.

One definition of "philosophy" describes it as an "attitude that acts as a guiding principle for behavior" so you're already well on your way.

There is a finite amount of time in every life, and no one knows how much time they have. Your philosophy of life can help you to decide how you feel about your existence and how you wish to spend the time your life contains. It reflects your attitude about your circumstances, and can guide your behavior.

You can consult a vast amount of theory, information, and advice on this. You might consider the philosophies of other people, the tents of different religions, or just the historical record of humanity—just to name three.

Give it some thought. What do *you* think about existence?

Let others walk their chosen paths

When you lead an authentic existence, your thoughts and words and actions all agree with who you are. This is an ongoing process, and we're constantly striving to improve ourselves.

We mean the things we say and we own the things we do. We expect others to allow us to follow the course we've selected for ourselves—which means we have to extend the same consideration to them.

Every one of us is unique. Some people we encounter will share many of our opinions and our values. Some won't share many of our opinions or values at all. That's a good thing. The world would be a dull place if everyone held the same set of ideas.

If we expect others to let us pursue our own authentic lives, it is incumbent upon us to do the same for them. We aren't obligated to voice agreement, but we are obligated to show them the courtesy we expect for ourselves.

Perpetual Rotation

As we go down life's road, the seasons keep changing and the earth keeps turning, regardless of what we do.

Rotation is a theme in nature. The young replace the old, who were once the young. Day follows night, and night follows day.

Very little is permanent. This can be both a comfort and a warning. In good times and bad, it's wisdom to know that neither lasts forever.

Living an authentic life can keep you ready for whatever comes down life's road. Your thoughts and actions will be consistent, no matter what happens, because they agree with who you are.

There is a value to adversity. We learn more from tough times than from easy ones. Those experiences serve as mental and spiritual signposts on the road behind us, reminders that you've bested or survived every challenge thrown at you so far.

You are still here, so make the most of it.

Make the most of you.

Related Reading

If you enjoyed *The Unused Path*, you may be intrigued to know it's featured in my futuristic fiction novel *A Pause in the Perpetual Rotation.*

That novel envisions a future United States where robots do just about everything. There is no need to hold a job, and no need for money. There are no corporations, just a few universities, and a non-elected government that runs everything.

Everyone has food, housing, clothing, health care, and police protection in the form of robotic marshals. The society emphasizes contentment and harmony, and anti-social activities can lead to long prison sentences.

The Unused Path plays a big part in that book. Embraced by different members of the society who are trying to give their lives meaning, it becomes the target of a government investigation that soon takes on a very sinister tone.

To learn more, please visit www.vincenthoneil.com.

About the Author

Vincent H. O'Neil brings a wealth of life experience to his writing. Over the years he has served as a paratrooper, a consultant, a risk manager, and an apprentice librarian.

A native of Massachusetts, he is a graduate of West Point and The Fletcher School.

His Malice Award-winning debut novel, *Murder in Exile*, was the first book in the Frank Cole mystery series from St. Martin's Press.

Writing as Henry V. O'Neil, he published his five-novel science fiction Sim War series with Harper Collins.

He's written two horror novels, *Interlands* and *Denizens*, and a theatre-themed mystery called *Death Troupe*.

His short fiction has appeared in numerous anthologies, as well as Escape Pod, Mystery Weekly, Hypnos, Bourbon Penn, Mystery Tribune, and Scene4 magazines.

www.vincenthoneil.com

Made in the USA
Middletown, DE
24 February 2022

61604886R00071